If I Had My Ministry to Live Over
I would...

Compiled by RICK INGLE

BROADMAN PRESS
Nashville, Tennessee

4227-04
ISBN: 0-8054-2704-X

Unless otherwise indicated, the Scripture quotations are taken from the King James Version. Quotations marked NASB are from the New American Revised Version. © The Lockman Foundation, La Habra, California, 1971, and are used by permission.

Dewey Decimal Classification: 253
Subject Headings: MINISTERS

Library of Congress Catalog Card Number: 77-78154
Printed in the United States of America

If I Had My Ministry to Live Over, I Would . . .

11/3/85

Mille —

" Praise God for
Your ministry) ;

Rich Dingle
phil. 4:13

DEDICATION

To the Lord's PREACHERS, who have known the heartaches, disappointments, frustrations, and mental and physical anguish of the ministry; yet, who count it all joy to *preach the Word* and serve our Lord Jesus Christ in the greatest work upon this earth, *"the gospel preaching ministry,"* I lovingly and cheerfully dedicate this book in the name of him whose "appearing" we all love.

FOREWORD

The idea for this book first came to me during a revival meeting in Birmingham, Alabama. Three months before, Dr. Robert G. Lee had been the evangelist in the church where I was conducting the revival meeting. I asked the associate pastor if he had picked up any "gems" from Dr. Lee? "Yes, one night after services I asked Dr. Lee, 'What are some of the things you would want to do if you had your ministry to live over?' Without one minute of hesitation Dr. Lee replied, 'I would want to be more patient, to comfort the saints more, and I would want to study the Word of God more.' "

It was from that tremendous statement that the idea for this book came. "What a tremendous blessing this could be to thousands of young preachers just coming on," I thought to myself. Then I began compiling the information contained in this book. Over three years of compilation has brought together some choice statements from twenty-five of God's choice preachers from all across America.

Dr. W. Herschel Ford was the second preacher to write

for me. Since that time he has gone to be with the Lord. This will make his comments even more precious.

I believe the reflections from these great men of God can be a tremendous blessing to all who read this book. May we read and learn as these, God's preachers, speak to our hearts.

RICK INGLE

Denton, Texas

CONTENTS

I Would Not Preach with Notes

1

L. L. Armstrong, *pastor*
First Baptist Church
Denton, Texas

If I had my ministry to live over, I would do some things that I have never done. If I had my ministry to live over, I would not do some things I have done. If I had my ministry to live over, I would begin sooner to do some of the things I now do. If I had my ministry to live over, I would rearrange the order of some of the things that I now do. And if I had my ministry to live over, I would do some of the things I now do, but would do them differently.

If I had my ministry to live over, I would begin by taking greater advantage of what was offered me in educational opportunities. The schools I attended and the teachers who taught me offered so much more than I accepted. If I could again be in the classroom and sit at the feet of the teachers, I would learn more than just enough to make a grade. I would recognize what they are offering as equipment for the ministry and that I need every bit of it. I would not only study the material

13

my teachers gave me, I would study my teachers and learn how they study and learn. I would learn about their study habits, their preservation of information, their organization of materials, and the tools that they consider essential. I would discipline myself to be a continuous student.

If I had my ministry to live over, I would listen more carefully and take heed to what my elders—those who have walked a little farther than I and lived a little longer—have to say. Instead of the painful experience of learning some things by my own experience, I would profit from theirs and save myself from some heartaches and frustrations. I know now, as I did not once know, that much heartache and time can be saved by learning from the experience of others. I would listen very carefully as they talk about crisis experiences that have come to them and how they have responded to them.

In living my ministry over, I would establish some priorities and discipline myself to live by them. I see this as necessary in order to keep from spending time and energy with things of secondary importance while first things go undone. One of the greatest frustrations of my ministry is that I feel myself forced to give time to that which I feel is not my first responsibility.

In establishing these priorities, I think I would first of all establish some "ministry" priorities. There are many things that demand the time of a minister if he is available. A pastor of a church of any size could spend all of his time visiting the elderly and the ill. He could spend all of his time in evangelistic visitation. He could spend all of his time visiting newcomers and prospects. He could spend all of his time studying. He could spend all of his time in administrative and organizational work. If I had my ministry to live over, I would arrange these things in order of importance, and my ability, and my time, and would devote attention to them in that order. I think this would be different in the lives of different ministers because of their abilities and gifts in different areas. I would, therefore, need to determine my gifts and abilities and my productivity in certain areas and arrange these priorities in accordance.

I would establish some "denominational" priorities. This would have to be done also in light of my gifts and responsibilities. I would try to determine the need for my ministry at the local church level, the association level, the state level, and the national level. Along with this, I would establish some priorities concerning institutional responsibilities, such as serving on committees, commissions, boards of trustees, and so on. In my ministry, I have been very grateful for our great denominational leaders who, while pastoring churches, have given themselves in service to great denominational responsibilities. I feel, however, that there is a great danger of ministers becoming great denominational servants while leaving the local flock unattended. I think if I were beginning over again, I would take a very close look at these different areas and would discipline myself to be of the utmost service in each of them.

There are also some "personal" priorities that I would establish. I would not accept any social, recreational, or personal engagements on Saturday evenings or on Sunday afternoons. As I look back at the days of my ministry, I am álmost driven to despair when I think about how I depleted my physical and mental strength on the eve of my greatest responsibility. I think of the many times when I needed to ask the forgiveness of God and of the congregation because I appeared before them at less than my best since I had been involved in things that could have been left off on Saturday evenings or Sunday afternoons. A preacher needs to be at his very best physically, mentally, emotionally, and spiritually when he stands before the people to preach the Word. I, therefore, would put aside those things that would drain strength and keep me from being my very best at times when I would be preaching. If I had my ministry to live over, I would take better care of my body. I know now that a healthy body is essential for an effective ministry. I would not want to come to the point the old man came to who said, "If I had known my body would last this long, I would have taken better care of it."

If I had my ministry to live over, I would give myself more to the enlisting and training of the laymen for doing the work of the ministry. I am now convinced that the lay members of the church are more willing and more capable of ministry than most ministers are willing to recognize. I feel that many who pastor churches try to do too many things ourselves rather than enlisting and training other people. I am convinced that a church that has everything done for it will soon be done for. If some preachers did not try to do so much themselves, the Lord would do more for the church.

In preaching, I would not take advantage of the pulpit

to castigate any individual or group. I would not use the pulpit to betray confidences that had been shared with me. As sacred as I regard the pulpit opportunity that I have now, I think that if I could begin my ministry over again, I would hold it even more sacred, and I would carefully guard it from the invasion of anything personal.

If I had my ministry to live over, there are two things I would do about my sermons specifically. I would begin as soon as possible to preach without any notes whatsoever. I have heard many people comment about preachers who preach without notes. I believe it is worth all the effort required to get a sermon so much on our hearts that we can deliver it without being bound to notes. Any written notes detract from the effectiveness of the sermon. There is no substitute for direct eye contact with the people to whom we are preaching. Perhaps right along with that I should say that if I were living my ministry over again, I would discipline myself to preach shorter sermons. I would not preach less gospel, I would just preach as much gospel in a shorter time. As I look back over many of the sermons I have preached, I see that there was injected into many of them material that was not really necessary. It was put there for entertainment or as a filler or for some reason other than a direct effort to communicate the gospel to the hearers.

If I had my ministry to live over, I would work very hard on my disposition and attitude concerning interruptions. I would learn to see and accept the ministry of interruptions. The normal response is fretfulness, irritation, or frustration. In one business establishment, it is said that there was a slogan that said, "A customer is not an interruption of our work, but is the reason for it." A member of our flock with problems is not an interruption of the pastor's work, but is the reason for it. I would try to let it be known that I am accessible and available any time to anybody under any circumstances to help them with any matter. This, no doubt, would sometimes prove to be a hardship, but the rewards of ministry would more than compensate for any sacrifice or hardship. Disregarding a minister's preaching, the one comment voiced by most people concerning their minister is that he simply is not available, or at least they do not feel that he is. I think it is important that we let the people know that we, their shepherds, are available to them, our flock.

If I had my ministry to live over, I think I would give more attention to my responsibility as a citizen. I do not think that the pastor should necessarily become a leader or that he should dominate the civic, school, and social affairs of the community, but I do believe that he should be interested and involved as a person. I would be careful not to let these things enter into my preaching ministry. I would be careful to function in these areas as a citizen and as a parent. I would try to so live in the community that people would recognize that the ministry is a high and holy calling, but that it is men who receive that high and holy calling and who, because of that calling, are not necessarily lifted out of or above the realms of responsibility of citizenship. While I would carefully guard against becoming involved in things that are relatively insignificant, I would determine the areas in which I could make a real contribution to the city that I am a citizen of.

In conclusion, if I had my ministry to live over, I would so live and minister that I could say, "If I had my ministry to live over, I would do just as I have done."

I Would Be More Positive

C. E. AUTREY, *former director*
Department of Evangelism
Home Mission Board

If I had my ministry to live over again there are many things that I would not change but there are several things that I would do in a different way and some attitudes I would change. I would not change my affiliation with the religious group that I have been associated with all of my ministry. I love them and what they are doing. When all is added and a complete summation is made, God has blessed them beyond degree.

I would not change my theology. I believe that God is a personal God and a personal man can contact him with personal faith. I believe now and have always believed that people can come to God on God's terms which are faith and repentance. I believe that when people come thus to God that they are begotten again—new creations. I believe that born-again people will work for God.

I would not change my evangelistic stance. I have always been evangelistic and have led all the churches

21

that it has been my honor to pastor to be evangelistic. My sermons were not all evangelistic because of necessity more than half of them were pastoral; but even the pastoral sermons were delivered within the warm framework of the outgoing spirit of God.

I would not change my pastoral practice. I have, in all pastorates, visited the homes again and again. I have visited the faithful to thank them and to encourage them to remain faithful to God to the end. I have visited the unfaithful members to cultivate them and involve them in the will and work of God. I do not go as a critic but as an undershepherd. I have visited the non-Christians. By going, it enabled me to break down the walls of fear, and it enabled them to be comfortable with me. At first I welcomed them to church and prayed with them. I have always urged them to let God speak to them and then make their decisions. After a time they would begin to ask questions and that enabled me to witness to them. I would never nag them, but I have and will go back to their homes again and again until they accept Christ by faith. Then I keep going back as long as I am pastor to cultivate and teach them in my limited way.

The young pastor who thinks that preaching the Word of God from the pulpit is enough should restudy the duties of an undershepherd. Great preaching alone will not be sufficient, and it never has been.

I would practice the love of God more. The heart of Christianity is love. When Jesus was asked, "Which is the great commandment in the law?" he replied, "Thou shalt love the Lord thy God with all thy heart, and with all thy soul, and with all thy mind [Deut. 6:5]. This is the first and great commandment. And the second is like unto it, Thou shalt love thy neighbour as thyself [Lev. 19:18]. On these two commandments hang all the law and the prophets" (Matt. 22:36–40). Jesus was saying that all God prompted Moses to write in the law, and all the law God had written in the conscience of men (Rom. 2:15) and all the prophets had said and written meant absolutely nothing apart from love. The love of God for men and men's love for God and people is the compendium of the law, prophets, and the gospel.

One's doctrines may be sound and his preaching dynamic, but if he is lacking in love for God and people, he may become contentious and thus stray from love and become dangerous rather than useful. If I could live my ministerial life over again, I would be far more charitable toward all people.

I would work at being more positive, and I would avoid the negative and critical attitudes as if they were deadly snakes. In my public ministry I criticized four men only and not by name. I have regretted it ever since. In the first place, I should not have criticized them; in the second place, all others in their category were made suspect. Thank God they did not attack me in return for making them suspect. I would say and do everything in a positive way and thereby be more helpful.

I would preach the Word of God more and give less attention to other things. "Faith cometh by hearing, and hearing by the word of God" (Rom. 10:17). I would depend more on the Holy Spirit. The Holy Spirit alone convicts of sin (John 16:8–11). No amount of direct and critical preaching can convict people of sin. I tried it, and I know it doesn't work! I wish I had learned earlier to depend more on the Holy Spirit. He alone translates Jesus Christ into reality. There is no spiritual power without the Holy Spirit.

I would have prayed more. One is never closer to God than when he is on his knees before God in prayer. A minister needs to be as close to God as possible. The challenges and problems of a minister are staggering, and without the nearness of God one may easily become frustrated and lose his purpose. It is not my intention to lead you to think that I did not pray many hours and days, but if I could do my ministry over again I would pray more. I would not study less but I would pray as much or more than I would study.

I would involve young people more. I was converted at fifteen but no one involved me in the work of the Lord and I drifted from the Lord from about seventeen to nineteen. Young people will not come and occupy benches for long. In my last pastorate I caught the vision of involving youth. I wish I had learned earlier. Although I am past retirement age, I am still pastoring. We involve our young people more now than ever. We begin with them where they are and lead them into more efficient service as they develop. If they play instruments, let them do so in the worship services. If they sing, let them sing. Place them on all committees and listen to them. The committees may not always follow their ideas but honestly listen to them. More than 90 percent of their concepts and suggestions will be new and workable and the committees will be wise enough to recognize this. Possibly the most potent human group on earth are our young people. They are enthusiastic, courageous, daring, and should be harnessed for our Lord.

In summation I would do many more things different if I had another chance. I could not have given more energy and time because I gave all I had, but I would have given it more wisely and considerately.

I Would Be More Patient with the Lord's People

3

CARL BATES, *pastor*
First Baptist Church
Charlotte, North Carolina

If I had my ministry to live over, I would likely make the same choices. Here are some things that I could wish would happen again. I could wish our heavenly Father would be pleased to let me have the same companion and the same happy child he gave us. I would like to attend the same seminary in the same period of time under the same great teachers who were there during my seminary days. I would begin my active ministry in the same way, on my knees with my wife in solemn covenant agreement to do two things: first, to preach his Word to the best of my ability, and second, to ask him alone to provide a place for that ministry and to stay there until he called me to another place and released me from my former place of service.

I would preach only expository sermons. I have tried to do this consistently but I would rely wholly upon the power of his Word used by his Spirit to accomplish his will and purpose in the lives of those coming under that ministry. And, I believe, I would always have hearers "under this plan."

I would do my best to indoctrinate every person who would sit still long enough to hear me. I would begin and teach a class for the new members. It could not be done in a few months or a few years. I would, therefore, hope to have lengthy pastorates.

I would not panic over the lack of visible results. I would rejoice if many people should respond openly, but if not, I would not "whip the church" until I had led the way in exhausting every means myself. Even if no visible results were seen, I would still know that our Lord would someday receive glory out of an honest effort on my part. In the meantime, I would keep in mind that I should be an example of one walking by faith and not by sight. I would try to remember the experience of Adoniram Judson.

I would be a better steward of my time and energy. I would not diminish my study time; rather I would increase it! I would permit nothing short of an extreme emergency to interrupt my study.

I would try to learn to preach with effectiveness. Every facet of the pastoral ministry is important, but I have learned that Baptist people will forgive almost every other failing in their pastor if he is an effective minister of God's Word. There are demands enough in the pastorate to keep a preacher on his knees in humility as he evaluates his ministry. There is work enough to occupy the time of three men; but, he still must learn to preach or he will automatically close some doors of opportunity forever. I find myself still dissatisfied with my efforts to preach after all these years. I still know that I need to know how.

I would pray for the Lord to let me be a pastor. It may be that one comes to love the pastorate only by "developing a shepherd's heart." I think that was one of God's gifts to me from the beginning.

I would be more patient with the Lord's people. I would try to remember that every member of my church began his membership in the church by confessing publicly that he was a sinner. It shouldn't surprise me if he acts the part; rather it should constitute a challenge for me to instruct him more perfectly in the way he ought to go. I would give up on him only when every means had been exhausted to bring him to spiritual maturity. Circumstances change; so do truly converted people.

I would encourage my church to have a larger share in the world's greatest missionary outreach—that of the Southern Baptist Convention! I would hope to accomplish this not by derogating missionary efforts on the part of other Christians, but I would try to help my people understand that we are doing more and doing it better in our missionary outreach than any other approach known to me.

I Would Keep a Prayer List of Lost People

J. HOWARD CLAYMAN, *pastor*
Washington Avenue Baptist Church
Evansville, Indiana

Praise to the Lord for the many blessings he has given me during my ministry. In looking back over my life as a minister, however, I find that there are two main areas I would change.

First, I would spend more time with my wife and children. As the head of my home, I would establish a definite program of togetherness by playing, vacationing, and having fun with them. I would give more time and attention to my children's problems, great or small, and to their interests. I feel in my heart that I have neglected my family.

The second main area I would change would be in setting an even higher goal for personal soul-winning. Early in my ministry, I found that I did not take enough interest in lost people unless I had a goal to reach. In setting a goal, I found that a desire was created in my heart to ask everyone about their spiritual welfare. Many times I asked individuals about their relationship

31

to the Lord Jesus before I really realized what was being said. The Lord has always made it possible for this goal to be exceeded. I have found that it is unimportant to speak of the number won through personal witnessing because, as the apostle Paul said, "For what is our hope, or joy, or crown of rejoicing? Are not even ye in the presence of our Lord Jesus Christ at his coming?" I have kept a personal record of those who have received Christ through my personal visitation ministry and they are a part of my prayer list.

It is important for a preacher to keep a prayer list of lost people. I have maintained such a list but have not depended solely on it. I have learned to seek the leadership of the Holy Spirit. One night I was visiting a family on my prayer list. It became apparent that they were not willing to accept Christ. After having prayer, I opened the door to leave and standing there was a man preparing to enter. That man accepted Christ before I left that house. In another instance, I was visiting homes of lost people without success. I asked the Lord to lead me. I was on a street where a person lived who was on my prayer list and whom I had visited many times. I felt impressed of the Holy Spirit to stop. That person was ready to accept Christ and did. On another day, I had a very hectic schedule. I asked the Lord to provide an opportunity for me to witness to someone. Less than fifteen minutes later, a man called requesting that I come to his home. Both he and his wife accepted Christ. I have found that in seeking the direction from the Lord, he will lead me to souls or will send them to me. Always depend upon his leadership. Let him change your plans.

I never get in a hurry when talking to individuals about Christ. In showing them about salvation, I always use the Bible, letting them read what God has said. After they have accepted Christ, I ask them to tell me what they have done to be saved. It is important that they have a scriptural testimony of their salvation. After hearing their testimony, I continue to show them out of the Bible that they have eternal life, but that when they sin, they should confess their sins to the great High Priest, the Lord Jesus Christ. They are shown that this confession is essential, not to keep their salvation, but to stay in fellowship with the Lord. They are encouraged to obey Christ in believer's baptism, uniting with the local church. I go back to visit them whether they come to the church or not.

Let me encourage every young preacher to spend more time with his family and to set a goal for personal soul-winning.

I Would Major More on Being Friendly to Lost People

T. T. Crabtree, *pastor*
First Baptist Church
Springfield, Missouri

If I had my ministry to live over, I would listen to the Holy Spirit more on a day by day basis and try to bring my life completely under his control.

If I had my ministry to live over, I would set for myself more specific goals of personal witnessing on a week by week basis. I would try to make witnessing one of the top priorities in my ministry.

If I had my ministry to live over, I would wish that I would be born in the home of my Christian parents and attend the same small rural Walnut Hill Baptist Church. I would again receive Jesus Christ as my Savior at the age of ten and surrender to his call to the ministry at age seventeen.

I would again attend Union University in Jackson, Tennessee, and the Southern Baptist Theological Seminary in Louisville, Kentucky. I would again marry the same wife, Bennie Elizabeth Cole of Buena Vista, Tennessee, who was also a student on the campus of Union

University. I would again serve exactly the same churches as I have had the privilege of serving now for more than thirty years.

If I could live my ministry over, I would spend more time in a devotional study of the Word of God, and I would spend more time in the throne room of the heavenly Father. I wish I could have heard Dr. E. F. Hallock speak years earlier of Bible study as being "the listening side of prayer."

If I had my ministry to live over, I would definitely plan for a day off every week and I would rigidly try to hold to those plans.

If I had my ministry to live over, I would give much more time and personal attention to my children than I have. I would spend much more time playing baseball and going fishing with my sons. This would have been good for them and for me, and I would have been a better pastor.

If I had my ministry to live over, I would major more upon forming meaningful friendships with unsaved men in order that I might witness to them more effectively.

If I had my ministry to live over, I would be more grateful to the good people who have been a real blessing to my life along the way.

I Would Seek to Hear the Great Men of My Day

W. A. CRISWELL, *pastor*
First Baptist Church
Dallas, Texas

It will soon be one-half century since I began my preaching ministry. Through these years I have learned many, many things. For the most part what I have learned is by corroborating the dedication to which I gave myself when I was a teenager. I became increasingly confirmed in my persuasion that the Bible is the infallible Word of God, that the Child of Bethlehem is the Savior of the world, and that Jesus is coming again to establish a kingdom that will never pass away.

If I had my ministry to live over again I would do these following things:

1. I would expound only the Word of God from the pulpit. It was after a decade of preaching that I began to take books of the Bible and ask God to help me open their meaning to the congregation Sunday morning and Sunday night. I would do this from the very beginning of my ministry if I could live it over again. If I could not get a sermon in a chapter, I would preach through five

37

chapters. If I could not find a message to preach in five chapters, I would preach through the whole book. However long the passage before me, I would deliver the message from that passage.

2. If I had my life to live over I would pray for God to help me crucify myself that I might live completely to the Lord. I would ask God to help me live above all the weaknesses that so often creep into a pastor's ministry. With eyes only for the approval of my Master, I would ask for strength to work day by day.

3. If I had my long ministry to live over again here in Dallas, I would start our Bible Institute years and years earlier. The members of our churches need deep study of the holy Scriptures. So many of our church leaders and church pastors need further and deeper study from the Word of God. The institute provides this training in a marvelous, effective way.

4. If I had my ministry to live over again, I would seek to hear the great men of my day, especially the great preachers. I had scarcely any opportunity to do this when I was a youth because I lived in such an isolated place, and there was little money for travel. Nevertheless, I would strive with all my heart to see and to hear the great men of God who were my contemporaries.

5. Needless to say, I always need to pray more, love God more, seek lost souls more, and serve our Savior more unselfishly.

IF I HAD MY MINISTRY TO LIVE OVER . . .

I Would Improve
My Platform Ability

H. Leo Eddleman, *former dean*
Criswell Bible Institute
Dallas, Texas

If I had my ministry to live over I would make no radical changes. I early "sought and found the pastor's heart." Though the last twenty-four years have been spent in higher education, practically every decision has been made with the pastor's perspective in mind.

If I could live my ministry over again, I would cultivate more the divine quality of compassion. It is the key word in the Christian faith.

I have endeavored to preach expository and textual sermons. This I would continue to do. As pastor I preached all the way through many books of the Bible such as: Ephesians for eight months every Sunday morning, all the way through the Gospel of Mark every Sunday evening for fourteen months, and so on. I would continue to preach expository and more prolifically if possible. Dealing with the Scriptures in a book by book study Sunday morning, Sunday evening, and even Wednesday evening for several months at a time, seemed to facilitate and motivate the spiritual growth of the people. This solved a great many counseling problems in advance. The people studied the Scriptures. When I stood to preach it seemed that all over the congregation one could hear "the rustlings of the leaves" of the Bible as people found the place for that particular message.

As pastor I made every effort to visit frequently. This I would continue to do. This helped me; it kept me close to the people and their problems and burdens. One afternoon during the second week of my ten-year pastorate, I made seventeen visits. The vice-president of an immense insurance company heard about it and invited me to lunch. During the conversation he said, "Preacher, is it true that you rang seventeen doorbells one afternoon last week?" I said, "Yes, but they were not all in, and I had to leave my calling card at five homes." Said this fine member of the church, "I have come to offer you a position with our insurance company. I don't have a man on my staff who will ring seventeen doorbells in an afternoon. If I did, he would have been rich by now." He proceeded to offer me over twice the salary that the church was paying me, with the assurance that after some months there would be a sales manager's position with almost pyramiding opportunities for material advancement. It was easy to say that my call to preach the Word of God was inescapable. It did not come with the accompaniment of jingling bells or flashing lights, but it was an irrevocable decision resulting from years of inner conviction.

One afternoon it was a privilege to take a fine deacon

visiting. During the third call, if memory serves correctly, a young, thirteen-year-old girl made a profession of faith. After prayer that the Lord would seal this experience with his Holy Spirit, we left. Walking down the sidewalk toward the car the deacon said, "Man, this is one of the greatest moments in all my life. Let us do this again." I said, "You are. Tomorrow you take deacon X visiting. You visit until you and he have had a similar experience either with some young person or some adult." This deacon did take another. The two of them had such an experience. Then these two took another deacon, and they visited until they had similar experiences. In less than twelve month's time almost twenty deacons were so committed to witnessing and visiting that I seldom stood in the pulpit to preach an expository sermon without the assurance that there were several people ready to make decisions at the conclusion of the service. This personal witnessing I would continue doing.

Every other year I taught nine study courses under the old departmental system of Sunday School organization. We usually began with the adults and worked down to the cradle roll. These studies would be Sunday through Wednesday night. They accomplished three things: First, the people would attend. With a total of twenty-three officers and teachers in the Junior department, it would be conspicuous if they were absent. The average attendance was over 90 percent in all departments. Second, it enabled me to get to know the people and their problems. Third, it made the people feel that I was sincerely concerned for them and their work. This I would do again if I had my ministry to do over.

In preaching, the ages thirteen through nineteen were kept in purview. The preaching was beamed to this segment of the audience. It was a privilege to have over half of every service under thirty years of age long before the population of the nation came to be approximately in that proportion. This I would continue to do. If a man gets and holds the attention of this age group, usually he can hold the attention of the rest.

In preaching to teenagers I attempted to have at least one good but new word that they almost certainly would not know. When using it, I always followed with an appositional phrase telling what it meant or stating it in synonymous terminology. The young people would consult the dictionary frequently to see if it had been used correctly. They sometimes quipped me about this. On one occasion a young man and his father said, "If you are going to give an appositional phrase explaining the meaning of the word, then why use the word in the first place?" The answer was, "If I do not use a word every once in a while that you people don't know the meaning of, then you will get to the place where you think you know as much as I do."

In 1950 Dr. Ellis Fuller invited me to teach in a seminary. For various reasons I felt it best not to resign the church, at least during the first years of teaching. I was in no mind to go into the teaching field. However, he said one day, "Eddleman, do you want to spend the rest of your life retailing what you have in a church, instead of joining us here where you can wholesale the gospel through students?" That got through to me. From that time on there was an intuitive feeling that God was leading me to the field of education.

The conviction grew that the field of education was my future. It has led from one exciting relationship to another. But education was no new emphasis. The church I pastored had more students in a Baptist junior college in that state than any other church in the state. At the same time it had more students in the senior Baptist college in the state than any church save one. A young lady from the church, about to receive her master's degree at Emory University, wrote, "Dear former pastor, As I stand on the threshold of receiving my master's degree I want to thank you for something you said once during the worship service when I was a junior girl. It motivated me to go as far as I could in preparing myself for service. You said, 'Young people, go and get so much education that nobody can ever look down on you. Then go get so much more education that you won't ever look down on anybody else.' " I would continue to encourage young people to seek more education.

Incidentally in the field of education, I found myself working as many hours as I had ever worked. But it was easier to control the hours in this area. One bit of serendipity discovered was the possibility of having more time with my family. Not that we had not already been a close-knit family in which the love ties were strong. As a family we would read together hours at a time some of the exciting literature of my youth. The works of Edgar Allen Poe, A. Conan Doyle, and others were high on the agenda. Of course this was in addition to the regular Bible reading we did.

Fortunately, the call into the field of education came just at the time when pastoral duties were accelerating to such a degree that I was not having as much time with the family as was desirable. I made up my mind to spend more time with the family and to get to know them well. In doing so, I found that my family are real nice people, once you get to know them. Both our children are girls. One is happily married to a successful attorney. The other is a doctor and married to a doctor and they are medical missionaries in Indonesia. My hobbies include such things as fishing, basketball, and volleyball—the kind of sport that takes me away from my family. If I could live my ministry over again, I would have primarily those hobbies in which my wife and two daughters could participate. I had the time with them as it was, but as sunset years approach, this is one of those factors which it seems should have been nearer the top of the priority list.

If I had my ministry to live over again, I would make everlastingly sure that both my family and I became fluent in one or more foreign languages. Actually, it should be at least one classical language and at least one or more foreign languages to be spoken within the family. This is not difficult. No one single factor, according to my observation, does as much to sharpen a person's mind and increase ability to think as the capacity to think and speak in another language. Having been able to do this mildly several decades ago, I nonetheless feel the intellectual lift from it to this day.

If I had my ministry to live over, I would study more.

I mean I would be more selective in what is to be studied. In college I majored in physics even though it was almost certain at the time that I would be a preacher. I earned twenty-eight hours in physics. There was a second major in mathematics which included twenty-eight hours also. Studying these gave me a measure of confidence at a time when science seemed to be riding the wave of the future. This confidence was much needed. Of all the subjects (besides languages) that would get attention, philosophy and philosophy of religion would come high. This assumes that one is already studying the Word of God unremittingly. Few things prepare a man to face a sophisticated generation like knowing philosophy, the terminology and ideology thereof. Incidentally, this is not foreign to the New Testament. In John 1:1 the term *logos* is but one of the numerous instances in which the Holy Spirit inspired a Bible writer to infuse theological life into an already rich and meaningful term. The idea of God in the abstract seems to appear first. But *logos* is a communicative term. So Christ is the great God of the universe reaching out to communicate himself to others. The response to this overture in and through Christ is elicited within us by the Spirit of God. The absolute oneness of God is matched by the trinity of personalities. This is not pluralism but a revelation of the functional role of each member of the Godhead in the plan of redemption. A fine woman recently finished a course in the philosophy of religion in Criswell Bible Institute. She said to me, "For the first time in my life, the circle of people with whom my husband orbits no longer makes me feel inferior. For the first time, when they bring up religion, I can answer them with confidence and in language that disarms them.''

If I had my ministry to live over, I would continue to try to ignite a flame of ambition in the heart of every young person. For example, at Georgetown College this effort was made. At the end of five years, many youth were majoring in physics, mathematics, languages, and taking Bible courses. In less than five years more than 54 percent of all those graduating in the senior class, were already signed up for master's degree work at some university or seminary. In turn many of these went on to secure doctorates. The only church I pastored, except student pastorates and in Jerusalem and Nazareth, was Parkland Baptist Church in Louisville, Kentucky for ten years. During the ten years at least thirty-four young people went into full-time Christian service who are still in it today. Of these, at least one third have earned doctor's degrees.

At both Georgetown College and New Orleans Baptist Theological Seminary, Mrs. Eddleman and I extended an invitation to every member of the graduating class every year to have dinner with us in the home. Most of them came. This I would continue to do. Even after the classes became so large that it was impossible to have them in the home even in small groups, we continued to have a special dinner with them prior to commencement at which time we attempted to manifest serious interest in their personal welfare and future. We received a blessing from them invariably and were able to pass it on to others. This helped to bridge the gap between the generation that was coming along and us. Both at college and at seminary, I sought earnestly to help locate work for senior students who were not going on for higher degrees. It was our privilege to help many who were in the ministry and also many who were not preachers.

We still receive letters of gratitude intermittently. Recently a Japanese citizen who graduated from Georgetown College wrote somewhat as follows: "Dear Dr. and Mrs. Eddleman, I have just now married. I was so long getting married because I was determined to marry a Baptist girl. It took me this long to find one. Never shall I forget the kindnesses extended me at Georgetown College. But the greatest of all things that happened was my conversion to the Lord Jesus Christ. Thanks again." In recommending young preachers to churches, I sought never to move ahead of the Holy Spirit. In every letter or telephone call, there was always a prayer beseeching the Spirit of God to bless the effort. If the efforts were not of his choosing, the prayer was that the outcome would be according to God's will whatever that was. This effort is still continued in the same manner. If I had my ministry to live over, I would continue to help young people locate work.

The awesome responsibility of an administrator in education beggars description. I asked a dean at one institution, "What do you think my major responsibility here is?" Without hesitation he replied, "Mr. President, if you do well the task of leading the trustees to employ good professors, then you will have served your purpose." This I sought earnestly to do. Always a prospective faculty member was assessed according to his professed loyalty to Christ, his inquisitive and curious mind, his cultural and intellectual demeanor, his ability to communicate, his humble and evangelical spirit. No one can bat 1,000 percent in this responsibility. But if I could live my ministry over again, I would seek as earnestly as before, and more if possible, to achieve these same goals.

Twenty-four of the happiest months of our lives were spent in Nashville, Tennessee, with the Baptist Sunday School Board as manuscript analyst. From one standpoint this is a phase of my ministry that I could wish to have occurred early in life. The reason is that that experience gave me a broader understanding of the awesome responsibilities of the executive directors, and presidents of Southern Baptist agencies. As manuscript analyst, my responsibility was largely one of "public relations" and denominational and literary accuracy as well as finesse. This was a most educative experience. Dr. James L. Sullivan is surely one of the outstanding administrators in the history of the Southern Baptist Convention. Few men have had as awesome and thorny a responsibility as he has had. It would be difficult to find anyone who could excel his ministry. If I had those twenty-four months to live over again, I would simply attempt to do the work more assiduously.

If I had my ministry to live over, including even the five years spent in the Middle East, I could wish for no radical changes. It was my privilege to be appointed by the Foreign Mission Board in the fall of 1935 and I arrived in Jerusalem in January, 1936. I was a single man though engaged to marry Miss Sarah Fox some twenty-one months later when she received her master of religious education degree. As a single man, I had far more time than would be true later. Accordingly, it was possible to learn Hebrew and attempt a first sermon in it some nine months later. Numerous missionaries in their approach to the Jews would begin with the subject of the return of the Jews to Palestine. This catered to their nationalism and patriotism, which already burned high enough as it was. I never used this approach. To the Jew it was, "In the gospel of Christ we have something far superior to Zionism." To the Arabs it was, "In the gospel of Christ and his kingdom we have something superior to Pan-Arabism."

Mrs. Eddleman and I were married in 1937 and located in Tel Aviv for one year. On buses and elsewhere we heard Hebrews boasting that not a single Christian lived in the city. The number of Christians we came to know was astounding. One of them was the brother of Jacob Gartenhaus. Many of them were "secret" believers. But they had a faith in Jesus Christ, and it was genuine. One said, "I was converted in Vienna, Austria. My wife and children were persecuted for my faith, a faith which they did not share. This is why I do not come out openly for Christ in Tel Aviv. I do not think it is fair for my wife and children to suffer for my faith in Christ. If I came out openly now I would lose my job in the public schools and my wife and children would go hungry." I did not encourage them in this status of "secret" believers. But on seeing the persecution to which they were subjected, it was impossible not to see their point of view. I would not change this posture.

Later the Foreign Mission Board asked us to pastor the church and be superintendent of the school in Nazareth. We did for about three years. Some of the most blessed memories of loyalty under stress, bloodshed in open street battles within a hundred yards of our dwelling and school, conversion of Arabs under adverse circumstances, linger. We went out one night against the laws of the curfew imposed by the British to succor a woman who had attempted suicide. Mrs. Eddleman precipitated regurgitation and the woman lived. On asking why she tried to resign from the human race, her reply in Arabic was, "I could not stand the thought of being the wife of a Moslem any longer." We did our best to encourage and console her in her circumstances. She had wanted to be baptized but her husband had declined adamantly to give her permission. The morning we left Nazareth to come back to the United States the husband of this woman came to our door before daylight. Among other things he said, *"Kaseese* (preacher), I wanted you to know before you leave that I have made up my mind that it is all right for you to go ahead and baptize my wife. By the time you get back I may be ready to let you baptize me, too." If I had my ministry to live over, I would not change things like this one whit. Mrs. Eddleman and I simply wish that it could be God's will to go on indefinitely doing these things.

If I could live my ministry over again I would, in one way or another, learn everything possible about platform performance. Some people are listening to preachers. What we say can be said far more effectively than most of us say it. The director of a major movie company heard me preach once in the First Baptist Church of Columbus, Georgia. After it was over we went out for refreshments. Among other things he said, "It was good but you sure do throw away a lot of punch lines." Dr. Othel Hand and I listened to him for nearly two hours as he explained to us what both of us could do to improve our platform ability. Preaching is the greatest business in the world. But the way we do it is by no means commensurate with the quality of what we are handling. Pulpiteering, platform ability, can be improved and it ought to be. New Testament churches today have a small amount of *koinonia* at the table on Wednesday evenings. A smaller amount of *koinonia* in Church Training. A limited amount in studying the Bible in Sunday School. But the point at which the *koinonia* of the church comes nearer being churchwide is at the Sunday morning preaching service. By all means this largest spread of church *koinonia* ought to be taken advantage of by the preaching of the Word in the most effective manner possible.

If I could live my ministry over, I think undoubtedly I would seek to praise God more. I would try to pray earnestly, regularly, humbly, thoughtfully, and beseechingly in behalf of others. But I have not praised God in a manner commensurate with his charcter. Our missionary daughter told me the month that she and her family visited us in Dallas before they left for Indonesia, "Father, I have found that no matter how trying the circumstances, if I but praise God, it seems to

brighten the day. I have found that in every cir-
cumstance, no matter how bitter or disappointing, if I
keep on praising God and thanking him for the good
things that still remain, I find that the day is better and
my mood and faith are improved." I had come to that
same conclusion some four years ago. The reason was
that I had come into a period of life wholly unantici-
pated, namely a period of suffering. I am not a good
sufferer.

But I have often preached that every fruitful Christian must either suffer or so discipline himself that his
life will bear the fruit of suffering. In December, 1973, I
was flown in an ambulance plane to New Orleans,
Louisiana, where Dr. John D. Jackson removed three
vertebrae and grafted three one-inch bone plugs from
my hip into the areas carved out. This same surgeon
some three and a fraction years before had removed
three discs. For the first time in my life, I was tempted to
leave the ministry, for if there is anything difficult to
tolerate, it is a "spineless" preacher. For eighteen
months, beginning in June, 1970, the pain was intense.
At times almost unbearable. I learned to praise God. I
learned to thank him for the good things that still re-
mained. This attitude and habit of praising God has
done more to sustain a good disposition and has become a source of encouragement to others more than I
ever dreamed was possible. Unless I interpret the New
Testament wrongly, the disciples had a praise attitude
all the way through. They prayed not for an easier time
or a bigger church. They prayed that God would give
them boldness to utter his word while he, the Lord,

stretched forth his hand to heal. Having gone through four years when every step in walking was an independent metal unit, no longer spontaneous, I have learned to praise God for each single step. Frankly, it has come to the place where each step feels real good.

If I could have nine lives to live over, I would wish them all to be in the ministry.

I Would Give More Time to Personal Soul-Winning

Roy Fish, *professor of evangelism*
Southwestern Baptist Seminary
Fort Worth, Texas

There are three categories into which things fall as I reflect on what I would do if I had my entire ministry to live over again. First, there are some things I did I would not do at all now. Second, there are some things I did that I would do much more of if I could do them over again. And third, there are some things I hardly did at all which I would do in abundance with another chance.

First, there are things I did which I would not do again. I would discourage my church from tolerating organization simply for organization's sake. Organization is a means to an end, not an end within itself. In my earlier ministry, I was guilty of making organization an end rather than a means.

I was always anxious to be a 100 percent "cooperating" Southern Baptist and always did what was recommended by the leaders of my denomination. If certain organizations or particular structures within organizations were encouraged, I always endeavored to begin them and to promote them. I did this whether our church needed them or not. I never stopped to consider that they might not "fit our situation." What I did was to saddle our congregation with time and energy consumers which actually were of little or no value to the kingdom. It did not occur to me that our church should have made a list of objectives we wanted to accomplish. In the first few years of my ministry, it never occurred to me that as a church, we should have had definite goals we wanted to reach; and that we should have encouraged or discouraged organization on the basis of whether the organizations helped us to reach those goals.

This would change if I had my pastoral ministry to live over again. My church would have its objectives clearly established, and we would jettison any organization which did not work toward helping us reach our objectives. I would encourage my church to let our purposes for existing determine the nature and extent of our organization.

As to things I did which I would do more of, there are several. First, I would be more consistent in my own devotional life. Prayer and Bible study have always been high on my list of priorities. But if I could live the last twenty-five years over again, I would give much more time to these vital disciplines. Instead of a few minutes, I would give at least one hour a day to prayer and devotional reading of the Bible. Instead of merely committing isolated verses to memory I would attempt to memorize paragraphs and chapters.

Second, I would give more time to personal soul-winning. This too was always a major emphasis in my ministry, but I would ask God for more boldness in making Christ known.

Third, there are some things that I did that I would do more of; I would trust God for more of his blessing on my ministry. Simply stated, I would expect more from God. Looking back on earlier days of my ministry, I am aware that I had trouble believing that God wanted to bless my work. This was due to the fact that I had my pronouns confused as far as my ministry and God were concerned. My thinking was, "God is here for *me* to use in *my* ministry." Needless to say, I was terribly mixed up on my arrangement of pronouns. Gradually it dawned on me that I had them backwards. I should have been thinking, "I'm here for God to use in his work and ministry." When I realized that the work is really his and not mine, it gave me reason to expect his blessing on his work in a way I had never expected it before. I realized that God wanted to work through me. Jesus said, "He who believes in Me . . . from his innermost being shall flow rivers of living water" (John 7:38, NASB). The flowing of the rivers of living water is conditioned on our continual trust in him. God wants us to expect him to bless his work in us and through us. For a long time I refused to believe this. If I had my earlier ministry to live over, I would expect more of God.

Finally there are some things I hardly did at all which I would do in abundance with another opportunity at pastoral ministry. I would major on the intensive training of a few laymen in my congregation so that they would be able to teach and train others. The Ephesians

4:11–12 concept never gripped me with any force as a pastor. I did not realize that God had given pastors to the church for the purpose of equipping laymen so they might find their place in ministry, that the body of Christ might be built up. If I had it to do over again, I would emulate Jesus who took twelve men and trained them throughly over a period of three years. Only after three years of training were they ready for real ministry. I would take a small group of men and pour my life into them. Over a period of months I would share with them everything I have. I would teach them all I know about Christian ministry. I would use every opportunity of association with these men for the purpose of teaching and training them. At the end I would have a small number of ministers in my church who could take a small number and teach and train them. I would train them not only in the area of effective witnessing, but also in how to study their Bibles, how to pray, how to live controlled by the Holy Spirit, how to walk victoriously as Christians, and how to be spiritual leaders in their own families. I would employ the principle suggested by the apostle Paul in 2 Timothy 2:2, "The things which you have heard from me in the presence of many witnesses, these entrust to faithful men, who will be able to teach others also" (NASB). I would major on committing what I have to faithful men who would in turn be able to teach others also.

Right now I am rejoicing in the fact that in all likelihood, I have much of my ministry yet ahead of me. I want to learn from the mistakes of the past. It may be that as you read this book you too are rejoicing that the final period to the story of your ministry has not yet been placed. You too might want to recommit your life and your ministry to the one who has called you for the purpose of more thoroughly fulfilling the reasons why he laid his hand on you.

I Would Give More Time to My Family

W. HERSCHEL FORD, *late pastor*
First Baptist Church
El Paso, Texas

I thank God that he called me into the ministry. If I am positive about anything in life I am positive that my call came not from friends or parents, or a church, but from God. This call was so definite, so clear, so moving, that I know it was of the Lord.

When this call came I was already married and trying by hard work to support my family. I had only two years of high school as my educational background, but from the way God helped me to get a college and seminary education and by the way he has blessed my ministry of preaching and writing over the years, I am quite sure that he wanted me to be a preacher.

I feel like Dr. George W. Truett, the great preacher and pastor, who said, "If I had a thousand lives I would want every one of them to be the life of a gospel preacher.

As I look back over fifty years as a preacher I can see a thousand mistakes that I have made. I cannot mention

61

many of them here, but simply write of several things I would change *if I had my ministry to live over again.*

I would make a deeper study of the Word of God. I believe the Bible to be the infallible Word of God, written by men who were breathed into by the Holy Spirit. I know much of the Bible, but I could have made a deeper study of all its doctrines and teachings. I could have saturated my sermons with more of the Scripture. My knowledge of the Word could have been greater with a deeper study, and my messages could have borne more of the truth "thus saith the Lord!"

I would pray more. Of course I prayed. I tried to stay so close to God that I could "pray without ceasing." Maybe many of my prayers were simple pleas to God to help me in my preaching and pastoral ministry. But maybe my prayers should have been more of simple communion with God. I tried daily to get alone with God and pray, but often I was too busy with a thousand details to do this. If I had prayed more I am sure I would have lived closer to God.

I would develop a more intimate devotional life. I know this is somewhat included in my first two points, but I would not have gone to the Word simply for new texts and fresh ideas, but I would have prayed and read the Bible more for my own spiritual enrichment.

I would develop a better memory. There was a time when I went to the pulpit with nothing in my hand. I read from the pulpit Bible and preached from memory. But then I was called to a church where I had to do everything but clean the building—and often I helped in that. I began to neglect the development of my memory and now I preach from notes. I do not use these notes slavishly, but I am afraid I use them as a crutch. Dr. Angel Martinez has memorized the New Testament and much of the Old Testament. I wish I had done this when I was young and had a good memory.

I would major more on the place of the Holy Spirit in a preacher's life and the lives of believers. The Holy Spirit was a greatly neglected matter when I was young. I am glad to see a renewed interest today in this all-important doctrine.

I would do more personal soul-winning. Some of the greatest trophies of grace along the way have been those precious souls that I have won to Christ in a face-to-face ministry. We preachers depend too much on our pulpit ministry to turn people to Christ. I wish I had done more witnessing on a personal basis.

I would be more patient with my staff. I was classified as a perfectionist, and I wanted everything done quickly and properly. I expected much of my staff, but many of them did not live up to my expectations. I am afraid that I sometimes became impatient with them and now I am sorry.

I would put more responsibility on my church leaders and take less of it upon myself. I knew because of my training and experience I could do certain things better than my leaders, so I pitched in and did those things myself. I got the job done, all right, but if I had laid this responsibility on my leaders maybe they would have developed into more effective servants of the Lord.

I would give more time to my family. Preachers feel that they must attend every meeting, counsel with every complainer, visit everyone with a "toe-ache," so we give our time to these things, to building up our churches, to making a success of our efforts. And in all of this we neglect our families. Maybe this is why some preacher's children go wrong: We need to have a public ministry of course, but we need to have a private ministry of love and attention and devotion to our family members.

I tried to be a good family man; my sons will say that I was a good daddy. My wife understood how much time I had to give to my work, but I can think of a thousand times when I could have put them before some other interests. These other interests would not have been greatly hurt, and my family would have greatly benefited.

Now as I come to the "sunset days," my one regret is that I have not been a better preacher and pastor and father and husband. But as I look forward to seeing Jesus I know he will forgive and forget all my sins and mistakes and shortcomings, and he will "understand and say well done!"

I Would Exercise More

10

C. WADE FREEMAN, *retired director*
Department of Evangelism
Baptist General Convention of Texas

More than ever before I would harmonize my life with New Testament teachings. I would move to live a life completely:

a. Characterized by the fruits of the Spirit: love, joy, peace, long-suffering, gentleness, goodness, faith, meekness, and temperance.

b. Characterized by purpose.

c. Characterized by the second mile.

d. Characterized by enduring faith and hope.

e. Characterized by self-discipline.

f. Characterized by sharing process.

I would always consider my wife's joy and welfare. I would provide the best possible inheritance for my wife and children. A good name is the greatest possible inheritance. I would adopt an asset goal to care for my wife and children properly.

I would adopt a goal to keep mentally, spiritually, and physically alert. The goal would include:

a. Mentally—have an open mind, read at least two books a month, develop a challenging study-program.

b. Physically—walk or swim daily, control eating and emotions, have annual checkup.

I would resolve to continue in the calling where I find joy and fulfillment. I would attempt to assist more people to a higher level in life through the sharing process and then through developing the capacity to understand people and their basic motives of emotions, love, sex, self-preservation, desire, freedom of body, mind, soul, self-expression, life after death, anger and fear.

I would develop the "big four" as my guiding principles of life:

a. Develop the habit of going the extra mile.

b. Establish a definite program.

c. Use master-mind alliance. (Use experts in developing maximum programs in both personal and business life.)

d. Combine these with faith, both active and passive.

I Would Schedule My Time Better

11

DAVID R. GRANT, *pastor*
Broadmoor Baptist Church
Jackson, Mississippi

First, assuming that I live beyond retirement age, I still have ten years to go: therefore, some of the things I do not like about myself, I am still trying to improve; and the things I do like about myself, I am trying to make even better.

If I had my ministry to live over, there are some things I would do just as I have done them. I would pursue my education as I did. I would acquire the same degrees from the same schools. I would answer the call to each church I served as pastor and stay as I have at each one of them.

I would make the same decision in choosing my life's partner. I would make the same basic approach to my overall ministry as I have. By this I mean, I would try to be a biblical preacher by preaching through many books of the Bible, dealing with various subjects of the Bible, and the great doctrines of the Bible.

If I had my ministry to live over, I would seek to be a

good pastor, ministering to the people the best I know how. I would seek to be a servant of my denomination as I have been called upon to do. I would seek to be a good family man by being a good dad and a good husband. I would make the same trips I have been privileged to make and take my family with me.

If I had my ministry to live over, there are some things I would do differently. I would try to memorize much more Scripture than I know now. I think I would memorize the book of Proverbs, plus many other passages.

I would start much earlier and work considerably harder in learning the skills of human relations. I would learn to deal with my own strengths and weaknesses, as well as with my relationship to staff, church members, and people at large. I would seek to learn a better way to schedule my time and set a pace that would be more in keeping with my ability.

I would seek to study more biographies of spiritual giants and learn how to have a deeper and more meaningful devotional life. I would seek to become more effective by spending more time in intercessory prayer.

I would develop a better skill in listening to God and committing all things to him.

I would try harder to be a real friend to my fellow preachers if I had my ministry to live over again.

I Would Be a Better Listener

12

J. D. GREY, *pastor emeritus*
First Baptist Church
New Orleans, Louisiana

If I had my ministry to live over I would not alter my conviction about the authority of the Bible, and especially its teaching on the divine call to the ministry. I answered God's call at age sixteen. I was ordained November 28, 1925. After nearly fifty years in the ministry, I know God called me, and I have not turned back. Furthermore, I believe in divine placement. God brought me to the First Baptist Church, New Orleans, May 1, 1937, and kept me in that post for thirty-five years and eight months, and I retired from that assignment December 31, 1972.

Furthermore, I would not "change partners." God gave me a noble Christian woman as my companion. From the day we married, September 16, 1927, she has been a faithful companion, a devoted mother to our twin daughters, a consecrated, capable Bible teacher, and an exemplary pastor's wife.

Moreover, there are certain basic things in my life and

ministry that I, like all Christians should and would desire to change. Among these would be to spend more time in prayer, to have a better devotional life, and to have more love for our Lord and people.

In reference to serving as a minister of the Lord Jesus Christ, there are some specific things I would do. If I had my ministry to live over . . .

I would read more widely. To be sure I read in preparation for my sermons. I read religious periodicals, news magazines, and newspapers. I tried to keep informed concerning my world. However, my reading on general topics not specifically related to sermon preparation was too limited. Reading the masterpieces of literature would have given me more eloquent terms for expression of thought.

I would write more. As a practice I did not write out my sermons. I made rather extensive notes and trained myself to use those without being a slave to them. I did write out addresses which I delivered at conventions and other historic or significant occasions. I also wrote my radio sermons for studio delivery. But it was done mainly to observe the time limitations. Had I written more, I would have published more books.

I would witness more. Early in my ministry, before the press of a large pastorate, denominational, and civic obligations, I did personal soul-winning nearly every day. But in the press of duties I let other things crowd this activity out, which was a sad mistake. I have observed that most of the pastors reporting large numbers of baptisms each year do so because they themselves witness, and their witnessing inspires the members of their church to also witness. Thus they become soul-winning pastors and soul-winning churches.

I would do more expository preaching. Most assuredly my sermons are biblically based and filled with a great deal of scriptural teaching. But it has been my observation that those preachers who stay a long time and build great churches are those who either preach through the Bible or have series of studies pertaining to topics or books of the Bible. Strong preachers and great churches are seldom built by exclusively preaching on topics of the day. Instead, strong churches are built by solid, expository preaching from the Word of God which "feeds the flock."

I would give more time to my family. Ours has been a happy, Christian home, and we are proud of our grown married daughters, but I was "so busy" that I left most of the responsibility of rearing the children to my dear wife. It was not true in my case, but I have known some ministers who "tore up their family while building up their church."

I would play and exercise more. As a boy, growing up, I never learned how to play. After school when the other boys went to football practice, I went downtown, got my papers and carried my paper route. In the evening, and in the morning I had paper routes. On Saturdays while the other boys were out fishing or playing sandlot baseball, I worked at a dime store straightening up the stock room or sweeping the floors. Forty years ago I played two rounds of golf. I never learned how to "hold the caddy." I realize now I should have learned how to play and I should have taken physical exercise. I am grateful the exercise gained by working when I was a boy gave me a healthy, strong body. The last job I had before I "quit working and went to preaching" was digging rivets in a boiler factory. But I think I would have been the gainer had I taken some time for recreation and physical exercise.

I would be a better listener. I was often criticized, and rightly so, for not looking each individual right in the eye and giving him my complete attention while talking to him. I had a way of glancing around him to see the next person who was coming up for a conference. I earned the dubious reputation of being aloof and hard to talk to. I wish now I had learned to concentrate more on each individual, even the youngest child who had something to say to me.

I would live closer to my people. I did this earlier in my ministry, before the demands of a city church and outside responsibilities crowded in upon me. But I had many deacons and young families in my church that I never visited in their homes. I tried to make up for it by sending a birthday card to each church and Sunday School member for the past thirty years. But I would have learned much and been a much better minister if I had been closer to them in a personal way. Dr. M. E. Dodd, my mentor in the ministry, said, "A home-going pastor makes for a church-going people."

I Would Continue to Cooperate with the Denomination

13

HERSCHEL H. HOBBS, *pastor emeritus*
First Baptist Church
Oklahoma City, Oklahoma

If I had my ministry to live over I would. . . . What a statement to probe one's heart and thoughts. Judging by recent publicity some would answer, "I never would have been a pastor." Or having found the role so demanding, "I would quit!" Neither of these is my answer. The fact is that as I search over almost a half-century of ministry, I find few things that I would change, but many things I would try to do better. This may sound like egotism. But rather it is the response of one who has had a happy ministry. It has not always been easy, but it has been carried on in the conviction that my life has been in the hands of God seeking always to do his will! However, if I had my ministry to live over . . .

I would thank God that I was reared in a Christian home, and would try to live as one worthy of it.

I would marry the same girl who through the years has been the perfect helpmate as a pastor's wife. We married while we were young. Recently I told her the only change I would make would be to marry her sooner. She reminded me that I would have been arrested for robbing the cradle!

I would continue to believe that the Bible is God's inspired Word, truth without any mixture of error. Through the years I have studied all the theories of inspiration and the writing of the Bible. They have served only to confirm my absolute faith in the Scriptures as being God-breathed (2 Tim. 3:16) and that "holy men of God spake as they were moved [picked up and borne along] by the Holy Ghost [Spirit]" (2 Peter 1:21).

For the last twenty-five years of my pastoral ministry I did expository preaching almost exclusively. Had I known what I know now, I would have done so throughout my ministry. People are hungry for the Word of God, for Bible preaching, not just preaching from the Bible.

I would continue to believe in God in his triune revelation. Once one accepts the first four words in the Bible, "In the beginning God," all the rest comes easy. Thus, I have never had any problem about believing in Jesus' virgin birth, atoning death, bodily resurrection, and second coming. Apart from seeing him as God in flesh for salvation, neither his life nor history itself makes sense. But believing this, all else falls into place. Therefore, miracles are not surprises, but are to be expected.

While I have always tried to rely upon the power of the Holy Spirit, I would do it more. Since he is both the Spirit of God and of Christ (Rom. 8:9) sent forth to do God's work, it is impossible for God's people to do this work properly apart from the Holy Spirit's power.

Furthermore, I would endeavor to teach my people the deep things of the Spirit. Because pastors have failed to do this, our people today are confronted with problems related to the Holy Spirit and his work without knowing how to deal with them.

I would try to be a better pastor. I have always tried to be a pastor to the flock entrusted to my care. But I realize that in many ways I have failed to do this as I should. The modern pastor is caught up in so many lesser things that he is in danger of neglecting the greater ones. It is so easy to make a "pop call" at the hospital where hearts are breaking, and then rush away to committee meetings. Thus we let the *good* become the enemy of the *best*.

In counseling sessions I would listen more and talk less. So often there is healing balm for troubled spirits simply in having a sympathetic listener. Of course, having listened, I would seek to speak words of comfort, encouragement, and guidance. Sadly, until it is too late, we pastors never realize how much our people rely upon us in times of trial.

I would do more premarital counseling. For years I have done this. But the prior years are lost opportunities in this regard. It is so much better to help married people avoid pitfalls than to endeavor to rescue them, oftentimes when the situation has become humanly hopeless.

I would spend more time in personal witnessing. Because of a long illness of his wife, a man owed many doctors. When asked how he was paying them, he replied, "I pay the one who is fixing to sue me." This explains the allotment of time by many pastors. They give attention to the most pressing matters. On the surface some things must be done today, so soul-winning is often put off until tomorrow or next week. The first thing one knows, weeks have become months and years, and one begins to excuse himself because he is so busy. But he is not busy about primary things, which suggests the next thing.

I would rely more upon lay people. One of the most difficult things is to delegate responsibility. Because of his training, the pastor can do many things better than others. But the people in a church will never grow into effective servants for Christ until they are given the opportunity to try.

One of the most unfortunate punctuations in the Bible (done by man, not by the Holy Spirit; the Greek had no punctuation except the question mark written like our semicolon) is in Ephesians 4:11–12. As it reads in the King James Version it seems that verse 12 lists the duties of the offices of verse 11. When actually it should read that the responsibility of these officers is "for perfecting [equipping] of the saints for the work of the ministry for the edifying [building up] of the body of Christ." Of course, the pastor must lead—but he must involve others in the work.

Most pastors, including me, do not expect enough of their laymen. J. B. Gambrell once said, "You can't get many men to help you kill a mouse. But you can get many to go on a bear hunt."

I would spend more time in study, prayer and meditation. I have tried to do it from the beginning, but even more the last twenty years. But I would do it from the beginning if I had it to do over again. A wise old preacher once said to me, "Most preachers are like wasps. They are bigger the day they are hatched than ever thereafter." His application was that when a pastor leaves the seminary he neglects his study.

Long pastorates are built upon firm study habits. The pastor cannot keep putting out unless he is constantly taking in. And if the people see the results in the pulpit on Sunday, they will respect the pastor's time for study, prayer, and meditation during the week.

I would continue to cooperate with the denomination. I have always belonged to and been the pastor of a Baptist church which cooperated through the various Baptist groups. But Baptists show their independence through voluntary cooperation. Churches do best what they do together. In all my years as a pastor the only pressure I have felt in working through the Southern Baptist Convention is the conviction that I should cooperate with my brethren. It has always been my conviction that I should serve my denomination best from the base of the pastorate. I believe time has proved this to be true.

I would also continue to serve my denomination in whatever capacity I should be asked to serve. If pastors do not provide leadership in the denomination, it will have little or none. I have always felt that when I was serving in some denominational capacity, I was also serving my church. Of course, there must be a balance between the two phases of work with pastoral duties having the priority.

When I get to heaven I will have many sins on my record. But I have never sought to be put on committees or elected to offices. Yet there are few positions I have not been privileged to fill. I am grateful to God and my brethren for this. If I had it to do over again, I would only try to do a better job.

Related to this is the fact that I would cooperate more with those of other Christian groups in areas of common concern but would not compromise my own beliefs and those of my denomination. In doing more of this in latter years, I have found that other pastors share in the basics of the Christian faith. Differences? Yes. But there can be unity in diversity. Organic union. Never! But Christian unity. Yes! In the keynote address at the first Baptist World Congress in 1905, Dr. John Clifford said, "We were Christians before we were Baptists."

In the overall I look back upon a ministry that was ever reaching forth but never fully obtaining. Yet I press on. I have retired from the pastorate. But not from the ministry! And I shall not retire from the ministry, but simply wait for the Lord to say, "It is enough." I shall hope to hear Jesus' "well done" because I have served him and I belong to him.

And I shall say to my blessed Lord in that day, "Thank you, Lord, for putting this earthen vessel in the ministry. Should you grant me a thousand lives, I would want to spend all of them as your undershepherd by thy grace." As Eugenia Price says, "I have always been unsatisfied with myself but never dissatisfied with Christ.

I Would Never Criticize a Man of God

14

JACK HYLES, *pastor*
First Baptist Church
Hammond, Indiana

If I had my ministry to live over I would try never to criticize a man of God or to sit in judgment against him. I would try harder to refrain from listening to any such talk about any of God's men.

I would try to bless those that curse me, love those that hate me, and pray for those who despitefully use me.

I would never want to sit in judgment or sit in the seat of the scornful concerning fundamental churches and schools.

I would want to bring God's people together instead of separating them. About thirteen years ago God spoke to my heart concerning this matter. I am sure he had spoken before. I wish I had listened better! If I had my life to live over, I would want to be less retaliatory, and leave vengeance to the Lord.

I would want to love my people more. I would want to "show" that love more. I would want to hate sin more, but love the sinner with an ever-increasing love.

In summary, if I had my ministry to live over, I would want to live more like Christ, to love more like Christ, to forgive more like Christ and to be more like my Savior.

I Would Want to Be More Grateful

15

LANDRUM P. LEAVELL, *president*
New Orleans Baptist Seminary
New Orleans, Louisiana

If I had my ministry to live over the two things that immediately face me are: 1) I cannot live my life over, and 2) there is a certain implication of regret attached to any such statement.

Let me clearly affirm that I have no deep sense of regret over having missed out on any of the good things life has to offer. As with the Old Testament writer, I can say, "The lines have fallen to me in pleasant places." God has been good to me beyond anything that I could have ever dreamed, deserved, or desired. Yet this statement is made with a certain sense of imperfection, for I do know something of my own frailties, foibles, and failures.

If, indeed, I could live my life and ministry over, I would certainly want to be more effective as a soul-winner. I can think of certain notable instances in which persons to whom I failed to share a positive witness for Christ have died in their sins, as far as I have been able to tell. According to the Bible, those persons who I knew, and to whom I could have witnessed, went out into eternity unprepared to meet the Lord.

If I could start all over, I would commit a greater portion of my daily schedule to Bible study and sermon preparation. While much of my time has been spent in dialogues, the greatest opportunity for the spread of the gospel came when I stood in the pulpit.

If I could begin anew, I would certainly seek to establish my priorities more firmly, and to arrange my personal schedule to allow for more time with people. My Lord spent a great deal of time in prayer and meditation, but he spent large segments of his earthly ministry in dealing with human need. I would want to be more like him.

I would surely want to be more grateful if I could live my life again. There are many to whom I could speak a sincere word of gratitude, and others to whom I could speak a word of praise for jobs well done.

To sum it all up, my one desire would be to become more like the Master.

16 | I Would Not Sign Notes to Help People Get Money

ROBERT G. LEE, *pastor emeritus*
Bellevue Baptist Church
Memphis, Tennessee

If I had my ministry to live over, or if I had my life to live over, there are many things I would not do differently:

I would. . . . marry the same girl I married. I would not change my belief and conviction that the Bible is the inspired, infallible, inerrant Word of God.

I would not dilute my hatred of booze. Booze is as bad as poison or sewerage in the drinking fountain, as bad as strychnine in the baby's milk bottle, as bad as poison ivy in the bride's bouquet, as bad as a mad dog on a children's playground, as bad as a rattlesnake in a kindergarten, as bad as a rapist in a girl's dormitory, as bad as a maniac wielding a razor in an old folk's home.

If I had my life to live over as a preacher:

I would try to be a greater comforter. There are so many sad folks and some with smiling faces hide a storm in the bosom. There are some who find that it rains when the sky is clear and snow covers the flower garden. Broken-hearted folks are everywhere—in little homes, palatial homes, in business circles, and in the political arena.

In my ministry, I did try to comfort all who needed it. My church members will testify to that. But were I pastor again, I would try to be more of a comfort—do better work as a comforter, and use the bandage more effectively.

I would not sign notes for people to get money because of my signature. In other words, I would not "stick my fist" to any note! That is one reason now that I do not use notes in my public speaking. I have signed so many notes and had to pay them until I have a distaste for notes!

As to "note signing," I was disobedient to God's Word, which says, "He that is surety for a stranger shall smart for it: and he that hateth suretiship is sure" (Prov. 11:15). The Bible also says: "If thou be surety for thy friend . . . thou art snared with the words of thy mouth" (Prov. 6:1–2). In other words, if I said yes rather than no to him who asked me to sign a note, I was caught in a snare. Some may say I was softheaded or grotesquely gullible. But if I had all the money I have paid on notes I signed for others, I would have over ten thousand dollars.

I suppose some of the preachers who would not keep their word as to payment on the notes I signed, are preaching occasionally on the subject, "Provide things honest in the sight of all men" (Prov. 12:17).

No Sir: No Ma'am: I would never sign a note—if I had my ministry to live over again!

I would exercise more patience. Paul wrote to the Thessalonians: I "glory in you . . . for your patience" (2 Thess. 1:4). For years, nobody could say that about me. Impatience was my besetting sin. I was not like the Chinese woman who, while rubbing a crowbar on a rock, was asked: "What are you making?" "A needle," she answered!

For years I could not stand for things to be put off until tomorrow, those things should be done at once— TODAY!

I would talk less conversationally. I have wasted time and the time of others talking—when their words and mine were not "apples of gold in pictures of silver." I have never done any dirty talking, but I have done some silly and careless talking!

I would do as I have done all along, I would respect myself. I cannot get away from myself. I eat with him and work with him. I can get away from everybody else but not from myself! Since I am with this man all the time and everywhere, I would try not to make him ashamed!

I would live as I have always lived as a minister, I would not be satisfied with what I have done. I would keep my mind's eye on what I am to become. Hence, I would and will put away egotism. I would not be angry when shown my shortcomings, but would study to overcome them! I would not get puffed up, but would try to build up. All along, I have tried to keep this attitude.

I would watch my thoughts. Realizing that thoughts are things, that they make and unmake folks, that they underlie success or cause failure, I would shut out all thoughts of failure, all morbid broodings, all fear, all despondency. I would shun all such thoughts as I would refuse to eat unclean food.

I would be absolutely honest both with myself and others. I would be honest in the dark as well as in the light, alone as well as in public affairs. I would look on any money made dishonestly as dirty money.

I would take care of my body. From my body, I get endurance, good spirits, pep, and vigor. I would never abuse it by excess. I would not cheat it by lack of proper rest and recreation. I would not let my body grow flabby from want of exercise. I would eat and drink intelligently—not as an indoor sport, but to keep my body fit. I would try to be "always bearing about in the body the dying of the Lord Jesus, that the life also of Jesus might be made manifest in this body" (2 Cor. 4:10). This I tried to do for years. If I had those years to live over, I would do my best in this matter of the body!

I would improve my mind. I would study hard every day. I would follow some course of reading and not fritter away my mentality on trash. I would study, study, study—put my mind to hardship in study. This I did and I would do again—had I the years to live over!

I would live with enthusiasm. I would never give way to complaint or bitterness. I would avoid pessimism and keep away from gloomy people as much as possible. Joy is an asset of life!

I would determine to succeed. I would believe that nothing could stop me, that I was wired to the central power plant of the universe. If one road were blocked I would make a detour, but I would get there! I would put every ounce of my strength into my work. If necessary, I would work night and day.

I would be more instant and constant in prayer. I prayed often during my ministry but I would do more. I rejoice in what Dr. R. A. Torrey said: "Nothing lies beyond the reach of prayer except that which lies beyond the will of God." Prayer is the only omnipotence God grants a human body.

I Would Begin My Ministry as an Expository Preacher

17

HOMER G. LINDSAY, SR., *pastor emeritus*
First Baptist Church
Jacksonville, Florida

If I had my ministry to live over, I would likely do very much as I have done because of my rearing, teaching, training, and the deep convictions and deep love I have for my Lord and his church. I was a prelaw student during my college years and did not surrender to preach until I had finished college. I married the right girl, and she wanted to be a pastor's wife. I came under the influence of her great preacher-father, Dr. L. S. Ewton who was the most influential man in shaping my life and ministry. My preacher-father was a great pastor evangelist who believed the Bible as the unerring, infallible Word of God, and Dr. Ewton was one of the wisest pastors who ever lived. I was fortunate to have their wise counsel over so many years. I was fortunate to come under the wise teaching and counsel of Dr. L. R. Scarborough and Dr. Robert G. Lee. These truly great, wise, and mature men of God did so much to shape my life and ministry. I thank my God upon every remembrance of them.

If I had my ministry to live over, I would try harder to be more like Jesus. I would be an encourager and never a discourager. I would show more love to my fellow Christians, and members of my flock. I would be a greater comforter. I would exercise more patience. I would be less critical of others. I would definitely cultivate a greater sense of humor. I would try harder to laugh at myself and see the funny side of things.

I would begin my ministry by being an expository preacher. I feel that I wasted several years as a topical preacher, and my ministry and my church was transformed when I began to preach through the Bible book by book and chapter by chapter. I discovered that my preaching was more balanced. The Bible never gets hung up on any one doctrine but moves from one to another. I really began to grow in my Bible knowledge, and my people began to love the Bible as the Word of God. I found there was a real hunger to know the Bible. I found that expository preaching appealed to all ages. I believe that expository preaching grows great churches.

I would have a quiet time every day and study the Bible for my own spiritual enrichment. I would spend more time in the prayer closet waiting upon the Lord. I would give more time to letting God search my heart. I would surely look to him more for the orders of the day. I would be more of an intercessor at the throne of God's grace.

I would do more personal soul-winning. God has given me many wonderful trophies over the years, but I am convinced there is no substitute for dealing with people one by one. Jesus took time to preach his greatest sermon on the water of life to one depraved woman, to the rich young ruler, and then to Zacchaeus, dealing with them one by one. Surely none of us are too important or too busy to follow his example. Soul-winning pastors develop soul-winning churches.

I would give more time to my family, instead of attending so many meetings to meet someone's standard. I would strive hard to evaluate everything and develop priorities. I would try much harder to be a good family man, to minister to the needs of my own family.

I Would Master One Book of the Bible

18

ANGEL MARTINEZ, *evangelist*
Fort Smith, Arkansas

Retrospect is a useful tool in assessing the past. One can survey the panorama of yesterday and determine what should have been done and what should have been left undone. The wheat and the chaff are mixed together in the harvest of life, and very few of us can distinguish the difference on the journey of human existence.

Life has no dress rehearsals; we take things as they come. And on the spur of the moment we act or refuse to act, and then, as one looks back, he can see the wisdom or the folly of his action.

One of the elements of our fallen nature is the inability to possess a correct insight into the present moment. We weep in the present about things that we laugh about later. We worry excessively about passing problems, and a year later we do not even remember what they were.

Casting a backward look, I can see things that would

have added effectiveness to my life. If I had a special second chance to relive from birth to fifty-four (my present age), I would incorporate the following concepts into my life.

I would master one of the books of the Bible. The minister needs to study the Word of God comprehensively, but one brief lifetime does not afford sufficient study to become an expert in all of the Scriptures.

I would take a book like Revelation or the Gospel of John or the book of Ezekiel and collect the best commentaries written in the field and become an expert in that specific book through daily study and repetition.

I would learn how to play a musical instrument. Every minister should know the truth and harmony as expressed through the piano, trumpet, or a stringed instrument. A few minutes a day invested in this relaxing art would bring a fruitful expertise to a man of God.

I would memorize the vocabulary of the Greek New Testament. There are 5400 words used to convey God's message to the heart of man. If the preacher memorized ten a week, in ten years, a brief span of our ministry, he would be able to extract the accurate interpretation of the Word of God. Bruce Metzger, the Princeton scholar, has listed all of these words in simple form, making them accessible to the preacher.

I would become an expert in a manual art. A few hours of study or tinkering experimentally in woodwork, electronics, or automobile mechanics would make the minister adept in a field different from his own. This would be very relaxing, and supplement with joy the rigorous intellectual activity that would characterize his ministry during a lifetime.

I would learn, and play well, one of the sports. Dedicated practice in golf, swimming, karate, or tennis would not only give one a great measure of recreation, but also provide a basis for establishing rapport with others in the exercise of the game.

I would read widely in one of the sciences. The investment of a few minutes daily in the field of astronomy, physiology, or geology, or some other science would give one a profusion of illustrations and win him the respect of those who study in various fields.

I would be more friendly. I would study the psychology of friendship and use it, not only for delight that a multitude of friends can produce, but for the purpose of witnessing for the Lord. Jesus was a friend of sinners. We who follow in his steps should be no less.

19 | I Would Sin Less, Speak Less, Study More

L. L. MORRISS, *director*
Department of Evangelism
Baptist General Convention of Texas

Sin less.

Speak less.

Study more.

If I had my ministry to live over again I would give myself to better preparation through formal training, faithful Bible study, and fervent prayer.

If I had my ministry to live over again, I would seek less to be happy and concern myself with being holy. I would heed the admonition of Paul: "Rejoice in the Lord alway: and again I say, Rejoice. Let your moderation be known unto all men. The Lord is at hand. Be careful for nothing; but in every thing by prayer and supplication with thanksgiving let your requests be made known unto God" (Phil. 4:4–6).

If I could live my ministry over again I would be grateful for the opportunity and ask his forgiveness for my failure to do these things the first time. I would plead with my fellow ministers: "Therefore, my beloved brethren, be ye steadfast, unmovable, always abounding in the work of the Lord, forasmuch as ye know that your labour is not in vain in the Lord" (1 Cor. 15:58).

20

I Would Visit More in Homes and Hospitals

J. HAROLD SMITH, *evangelist*
Fort Smith, Arkansas

If I had my ministry to live over, I would certainly make many changes. I would not make many of the mistakes I have made. Hindsight is surely better than foresight. I would endeavor to memorize the entire Bible. I would master the Hebrew and Greek languages. I would diligently try to be more loyal, humble, and obedient as a servant of God. There would be less self and more of the Savior in every message.

Without doubt I would be more fearless in my declaration of the truth and more conscious of the judgment seat of Christ. I would attempt to please men less and seek earnestly only the approval of God upon my life, lip, light, liberty, and love. I would love the souls of all men regardless of race, religion, or riches. I would look upon every human being through the Scripture window of John 3:16.

To live daily with a consuming passion to see souls saved, backsliders reclaimed, and saints built up in a more holy faith, would be my desire if I could relive my ministry. I would spend more time on my knees in earnest prayer seeking God's wisdom in rightly dividing the Word and for greater power in preaching that Word.

I would be pleased to pastor the same churches where God has allowed me to serve. I would delegate more authority and responsibility to my laymen. I would be much kinder to the weak lambs, and would use stronger force against all wolves adorned in sheep's clothing. I would not tolerate or even show any sympathy for heresy. I would visit more in the homes and hospitals, and be more sympathetic in times of sorrow. I would try desperately to have a better understanding of the major problems of the individual members of my congregation.

If I had my ministry to live over I would make no changes in my call to preach the gospel of Christ, my choice of a godly wife, or the churches where God has allowed me to witness for him. I would make no changes in my approach of presenting the gospel of Christ by radio, TV, and the printed page to all men everywhere. I would only use them more.

If I had my ministry to live over, I would want to work more in the Spirit and less in the flesh; and let the Holy Spirit lead in all my decisions.

As I face the homestretch of my life and ministry, and approach that moment when I shall meet Christ face to face, if I could live my life all over again, I would seek to be a better husband, spend more time with my family, be a better neighbor, laborer, evangelist, preacher, and pastor. I would do my best to "love the unlovely," and go deeper into the byways and the hedges seeking the lost. I would be more concerned over the prodigals in the churches where I pastor. I would have but one ambition and that would be to hear my Lord say, "Well done, thou good and faithful servant."

21 | I Would Give Prayer and Fasting Absolute Priority

JACK TAYLOR, *evangelist*
Fort Worth, Texas

If I had my ministry to live over. . . . What a sobering supposition! It has driven me to reevaluate every facet of my ministry. For if there are things that I would do if I had my ministry to live over, I should do them now immediately! (If that is possible.) I have the privilege of looking toward the future. My observations are at once a cry of regret and a cry of determination. Regret that these were not a part of my ministry from the beginning and determination that from this moment on they will be!

I would give prayer absolute priority. I have always known prayer to be important. When I was just a young Christian, I learned that God answered prayer and I believed God in childlike faith. When time came to go to school, it seemed that learning shoved prayer to a lesser position of importance in my life. It was one of those things that could wait, so it seemed. Lessons had to be gotten. Classes had to be attended. Appointments had to be met. The ministry was getting busier and busier. In the back of my mind I never stopped believing in prayer's importance, and I suppose I felt that around the next bend when things slowed down I would have more time to pray. I have discovered one vital lesson. One never finds more time to pray by waiting on business to lessen! He must give prayer a position of priority!

I would not only give prayer a place of priority in my personal life but I would emphasize the priority of prayer in the life of the church. I would lead in the establishing of a full-blown prayer ministry with responsibilities and training as clear and definite as responsibilities to teach, visit, and witness. Jesus said, "My house shall be called of all nations the house of prayer . . . ye have made it a den of thieves."

I would explore and experience the value of fasting with prayer. Not until the last few years have I experimented with the matter of fasting. I had always heard about it but had never practiced it though I believed in it. So manifold are the advantages and blessings that accrue to the experience of fasting that I am amazed that I have been kept from it by my carelessness so long!

Fasting helps put *food* and *faith* in proper perspective. I should eat to live; not live to eat! Too much food limits the body and dulls the mind and ruins the testimony. Overeating will shorten the life and overwork the heart. I would deliberately take control over my body by refusing to let my physical being tell me what to do. I would fast regularly for spiritual and physical purposes and at times extend the fast into several days when occasions of spiritual need arose.

I would criticize preachers less and comfort preachers more. My ministry began with a competitive spirit. I have been since my boyhood a competitor. I wanted to excel! I believed that the success of my ministry would mean that I would outdistance the brethren! That is a lie from the devil. Now I realize that success is being a blessing to all in the name of Jesus. During the early years of my ministry I had the devilish inclination to criticize my preacher brothers. I realized later that it was because of insecurity in my own ministry. God has in these late years given me an undying love for preachers. I want to encourage them, lift them up, and help them. Never has there been a day when preachers were more in need of encouragement than today.

I would practice the secret of giving which is made so clear in the word of God. I have tithed since my ministry began. I thought that was enough. I have since discovered that this was only the beginning. I had-stopped at the beginning. Jesus said, "Give and it shall be given unto you; good measure, pressed down, and shaken together, and running over, shall men give unto your bosom. For with the same measure that ye mete withal it shall be measured to you again." If I had just believed in that with all my heart from the beginning of my ministry. How much more would have been in the coffers of missions for the winning of souls! How much more would my family have enjoyed of God's prosperity! How much would I have been able to share along the way with people who needed to go on with the Lord with their material possessions!

I would have practiced revelation giving instead of reason giving. For years I gave according to what I could afford beyond the tithe. Then I discovered that we are to give with the riches of God in mind. "God is able to make all grace abound toward you; that ye, always having all sufficiency in all things, may abound to every good work." Think of it—every good work! Too many times I have said, "I just can't afford it!" All this time the riches of the Lord were waiting to be poured out on me and through me to the world! I have discovered this principle to work in everything . . . time, love, concern, helpfulness, as well as money!

I would emphasize principles of personal health such as proper eating, resting, exercise, and discipline. For many years I considered it a mark of spirituality to drive my body to the breaking point. I thought it was a sign of true nobility. Now I conceive it to be foolishness! I would make a study of proper eating habits and proper foods with their natural values retained as much as possible. I would seek the advice of a competent physician as much as possible. I would seek advice as to the needs of the body over the years for vitamins, and so on. I would pass this information on to people whose health picture would change if they would believe and practice the principles of sound health. I would develop a taste for that which I knew to be good for me, not just that which tasted good to my taste buds.

I would learn more about the devil and his emmissaries the demons and of my rights in Jesus' name over them. For the greater part of my ministry I thought the devil and his demons were to be ignored, and not re-sisted. Ignoring them was precisely what I did until I found out that this was exactly what they wanted! I would not go overboard on the doctrine but I would get on board the vehicle of scriptural truth about the unseen world of evil as well as the world of angelic ministers. I was so afraid of getting out on a limb for years that I wouldn't even climb the tree of truth. I was so afraid of going overboard that I never got on board!

I would give a healthy, balanced, and scriptural em-phasis to spiritual gifts. Fear closed the door to this area of truth for years to me. A fearful overemphasis of certain gifts drove me to a nonemphasis on gifts in general. Every Christian has some! Few, if any, have all! None are signs of spirituality but of the grace of God. Our doing nothing has caused error to thrive and mal-practice to abound!

I would give exclusive attention to expository preach-ing. There are three types of sermons: topical, textual, and expository. I sought for years of my ministry to employ all three. This may be good but far and away expository preaching is the need of our day! I would develop the art of exposing a passage of Scripture, get-ting all points and subpoints from the passage.

I would be a pastor to my immediate family first. One of my greatest failures in the early part of my ministry was the neglect of my family. I was deceived into believ-ing that if I was busy within the context of my ministry surely God would overlook my neglect to my family and make up for it! I found out later that this was no excuse! My family deserves a pastor. If I am not their pastor, they will not have one and I will be the means of robbing them of that privilege! I would give the family priority.

I would be filled with the Spirit. I would allow the Holy Spirit office space to do his office work in my life and ministry. I would seek to place as a priority emphasis for Christian service the matter of being filled with the Spirit. I would place it before education, experience, persuasiveness, style, and study. It is not by might, nor by power but by the Spirit of God that the work of the ministry to which he has called us is performed!

Since I would do these things if I had my ministry to live over, I here and now confirm that to the best of my ability of the life that is within me I am giving myself to these convictions. God being my helper, the remainder of my years of ministry will find these qualities present!

I Would Still Want to Pastor One Church for Thirty Years

22

W. O. Vaught, Jr., *pastor*
Immanuel Baptist Church
Little Rock, Arkansas

Often across the years I have heard many ministers tell how they fought the call to the ministry. That was not my experience. From my earliest youth, even before my conversion, I knew that I was going to be a Baptist preacher. I was converted very young, in fact I was a Christian several years before I joined the Baptist church in Brooksville, Mississippi, at the age of eight. When I was a tiny little boy, I lived in Versailles, Kentucky, and some of the great professors from the Southern Baptist Seminary would stop by our home as they were going to their preaching assignments. Quite often I would climb up on their lap and tell them that I was going to be a Baptist preacher when I grew up, and that one day I was going to attend the Southern Baptist Seminary.

My call to the ministry and my conversion came together. My father and mother were great Christians, and I do not believe anyone could have grown up in my

109

home without being a Christian. I describe my conversion in this way. One day as I was walking along with my father, he just slipped my hand out of his and slipped it into the hand of Jesus and I hardly realized when the shift was made. I do not mean that I did not have a real genuine conversion. I not only had a genuine conversion, but I have never had one moment's doubt about my conversion. Therefore, I deserve no credit for the fact that I am a Christian and that I am a Baptist preacher. Both of these things came to me by the grace of God, and I have just watched them develop with amazement and praise.

I held my first small pastorate at the Topisaw Baptist Church, which was near Brookhaven, Mississippi, while I was a student at Mississippi College. When I finished college and went to the seminary in Louisville, Kentucky, I was called to two part-time churches at Salvisa and Cornishville, Kentucky. I pastored these two churches for the three years that I attended the seminary. Upon the completion of my work at the seminary in May, 1935, I became the Baptist student secretary for the state of Missouri, and continued in that task until 1940. My call to that work was indeed a call from God. As I came to the end of my seminary work, I had three offers before me. One was an offer from a church in Mississippi, another was from a church in Washington, D.C., and the third offer was from the Missouri Executive Board to be their Baptist student secretary. As though God had taken a pen and had written in red ink across that letter from Missouri, that call could not have been more definite. God said to me, "This is it!" and I knew that was my call.

After five years as Baptist Student Secretary, I became pastor of the Bethany Baptist Church in Kansas City, where I preached for two years. Then I moved to the University Baptist Church in Abilene, Texas, and pastored there for three years. In April, 1945, I came to the Immanuel Baptist Church of Little Rock, Arkansas, and I have been pastor here for thirty-two years.

If I had my ministry to live over again, I would blend the following principles into my life.

1. I would listen to God's call exactly as I did.
   Three times God has spoken to me very definitely and has always used the same words—"This is it!" I have never served in any place without being conscious of the fact that I was within the circle of God's direct will. I have often said to student groups and to many others, "To know the will of God is the greatest knowledge, to find the will of God is the greatest discovery, and to do the will of God is the greatest achievement!"

2. I would form the same prayer habits for my life.
   Mr. S. D. Gordon came to our great southwide Baptist student meetings and inspired us with his devotion to God and to prayer. I heard him say, "You cannot do more than pray, until you have prayed." He said, "Prayer is winning the victory over the devil; service is gathering up the results of victory after you have already won it." I determined then that I would form daily habits of prayer. Forty years ago I began to give the first hour of the day to meditation and prayer, and with

few exceptions, it has been my daily habit since then.

3. I would not change the glory that has come from a long pastorate.

Though I have been often tempted to leave my present pastorate, I thank God that his will has kept me at this task. There are so many glorious blessings that accrue from a long pastorate that one must experience in order to understand. If I had it to go over again, I would ask God to let me spend these last thirty-two years in this same place. Now, just past sixty, I am in the height of my ministry and the spiritual victories are increasing with every passing day.

4. I would not change the way we reared our son.

Mrs. Vaught and I consider ourselves fortunate indeed that we were able to rear a son who has respect for the church and the ministry. We count it one of God's greatest joys that our son was never rebellious, never deserted the early profession he made of his faith in Christ, and is today a Christian father and teacher.

On our twentieth anniversary here at Immanuel, he wrote a letter to the church from Yale University, where he was completing his work for a Ph.D. in philosophy. The concluding paragraph of that letter was as follows:

Finally, and most personally, I recognize that my father and mother have avoided the one grave mistake which so many preachers' families make—to have succeeded grandly in a church, first at the expense of each other, secondly at the expense of a son. To gain a church or indeed the whole world is a dubious honor when weighed against the loss of a family. That they have avoided this dreadful mistake might well have been their greatest achievement. If for no other reason than this, my wife and I would join you with great pleasure and happiness in honoring your pastor and his wife on the occasion of their twentieth anniversary at Immanuel.

5. I would change my early evaluation of the worth of the study of Hebrew and Greek.

Though I took Greek and Hebrew at the seminary, I did not give diligence to the mastery of these languages. If I had to go to seminary again, I would study these languages until I could interpret the Scriptures right out of the original languages. Only in recent years have I returned to a daily study of Hebrew and Greek, and it has blessed my preaching ministry beyond anything I can say.

6. I would never preach a topical sermon.

For the early years of my ministry, I preached topically. I would spend half of my time reading sermon books and gathering illustrations to fit the topic I had selected for my sermon. About eight years ago I turned from this type of preaching, and I began to preach only Scripture, line by line, verse by verse, book by book. This has been the most important decision of my ministry. Bible preaching has changed my life, has changed my church, and has changed the lives of the thousands who have heard me. Such great excitement has come to my church because of Bible preaching that people now come to church with great excitement and expectation. All who now hear me preach bring a Bible, and they open it and follow along as the Scripture is explained. Our color television audience throughout the state of Arkansas has greatly increased and many thousands now share in these biblical messages. If I could start my ministry over again, this is the big change I would make. The Bible is the mind of Christ, according to 1 Corinthians 2:16, and I would spend all my time trying to let the people know the mind of Christ.

7. I would try to love preachers more.

I do not mean that I have not loved my preacher brothers. I have. But I would try harder to love them, work with them, and show more genuine concern for them and their work.

8. I would be a loyal Southern Baptist just as I have tried to be.

I am proud that I am a Southern Baptist. I am a denominationalist. I believe in denominations. I know God picked me out to be a Southern Baptist, and I am glad that I have given my efforts inside the structure of my denomination. Southern Baptists are not perfect, but I believe they are the best denomination on the earth, closer to the truth of the Word of God, and the most productive denomination in God's kingdom. I am thankful to be a Southern Baptist, and if I had it to do over, I would align myself with them just as I have done.

I Would Want to Develop More Personal Soul-Winners

23

JAROY WEBER, *pastor*
First Baptist Church
Lubbock, Texas

If I had my ministry to live over, I would have so many improvements to make that this book does not contain an adequate space for me to enumerate them. There are many areas which would ring with sentiment and nostalgia, such as an improvement as husband, father, and pastor.

No man with the spirit of Christ in him could feel that he has been his maximum in any area of responsibility.

As I think of my call from God to be a preacher of his Word, I feel that my greatest contribution to the kingdom of God would be to develop more personal soul-winners. Since we all know that it is the main thrust of the biblical revelation and really the heartbeat of our heavenly Father we should preach, write, and talk about the subject more than any other. The basic problem is we do little about it personally and we train few people in our lifetime. If I had my ministry to live over, I would spend more time in trying personally to relate

115

men to God through Jesus Christ, and I would develop some lay people who could become effective in personal evangelism.

If I were to live my ministry over, I would try to teach my people the concept of the church being the body of Christ and how each member is a vital part of the whole. This would give meaning and significance to every member of the congregation regardless of their background, training, or education. I would teach them that God has given each and every one of them a special gift which should be used to minister to the body. When used it will equip the body to be healthy so it can carry out the purpose of Christ in world evangelism. I feel this concept is from the New Testament, but it has been neglected by most of our ministries. Our people have not seen themselves as a cooperating fellowship in whom God dwells and through whom God is working to fulfill his purpose in world redemption. All problems of fellowship and discipleship are resolved when Christians have this concept of one body, many members, all equipped to give themselves totally to the work of Christ.

If I had my ministry to live over I would try to develop a more optimistic spirit and help other pastors to do likewise. I would realize, that as a God-called minister, my only responsibility is to stay in fellowship with Christ. When I am in proper fellowship with him, it is his responsibility to do his work through me and produce the desired results. I am not responsible for success, crowds, churches to pastor or visible results. It is the work God must do through his Spirit and I must not act or react as if these were my responsibilities. Living and serving in the power of the Holy Spirit and leaving the results to God will keep me and every minister with a better attitude and spirit than he could possibly have otherwise.

If I had my ministry to live over I would develop a more Christlike attitude. People where you preach will not remember your sermons, your stories, or your jokes, but they will remember your attitude. Our attitude is the biggest thing about us and makes the most indelible impression and influence upon people we serve. Let this be Christlike and you will always be remembered as the kind of pastor who fulfilled the mission of Christ. I would try to develop my attitude to be more Christlike if I had my ministry to live over.

I Would Earn My Doctor's Degree

24

JAMES P. WESBERRY, *pastor emeritus*
Morningside Baptist Church
Atlanta, Georgia

It is very difficult to know what I would do if I had my ministry to live over. From the very moment that I yielded to God's call to the gospel ministry I laid everything I ever dreamed of on his altar. I sought absolutely and completely to follow his will for my life and ministry. I did many things that did not seem logical. For one thing, I left my native state to go to a Baptist university in a neighboring state. My pastor did not seem to understand. But the Lord led. I went to New England to the seminary. That seemed so strange to many people, yet no one ever prayed harder or sought the guidance of God's Holy Spirit more than I. My life was committed as nearly one hundred per cent as I knew how to commit it. As odd as it may have appeared to others, I know that God was guiding me.

God has led me all the way. Some of the largest and best churches that ever called me were what I dreamed of all of my life, but when I tried to go I was blocked. I

119

declined a church of 3600 members to spend thirty-one years with a church that had only a temporary building and a little over 500 members when we began. That all seemed so unusual but as I look back, I know God's hand led me all the way. I have had a long, glorious, and happy ministry.

At the age of seventy I have never had so many open doors. I thank God for opening the door for me to serve as executive director of the Lord's Day Alliance of the United States and as editor of *Sunday* magazine. It never occurred to me that I would be in this position, with happy interim pastorates, pulpit supplies, and an abundance of other work.

The Lord does work in mysterious ways. If we give him our best, the best will always come back to us. I could not ask God for more. I have had many honors. I am in all the Who's Whos and have four honorary doctor's degrees, along with a long string of diplomas and citations. I have the most wonderful wife in the world and am blessed with a fine family.

I have 375 to 400 dear old people in a nearby nursing home where I have served for over thirty years. For thirteen years I was president of the board of managers for the nursing home. I visit them often. I love everyone of them. They help keep me young.

But, if I had a chance to do it over again, and if the Holy Spirit permitted it, there is one thing I think I would do that I am sorry I did not do. I would go to our seminary in Louisville and stay there until I earned my own doctor's degree.

A proud mother-in-law whom I visited was bragging

on her son-in-law having received his doctor's degree from the Southern Baptist Theological Seminary. Then she asked me, "Dr. Wesberry, where did you go to school?" I thought I would have a little fun, so I said, "I am sorry to tell you but I didn't get as much education as I wanted to." She then changed her whole attitude and with a kind look of sympathy said, "Well, you certainly are doing all right."

But, even though God has let me do all right and I owe it all to him, if I had it to do over and the Lord would let me, I would take the time to earn my own doctorate.

I Would Want to Have Closer Fellowship with Younger Preachers

K. Owen White, *pastor emeritus*
First Baptist Church
Houston, Texas

Paul said, "I thank Christ Jesus our Lord, who hath enabled me. . . . putting me into the ministry." This is my testimony. It had to be true in my case. He literally put me into the ministry. I was the most unlikely of all candidates. I was a country boy without even a high school education. I did not have the privilege of attending an organized Sunday School or church until I was past sixteen years of age. By nature I was timid and retiring.

The call came suddenly and unexpectedly. In my case God used a layman who simply said quietly one day, "Owen, have you ever thought of becoming a preacher?" My response was to say in astonishment, "Who? Me?" He replied, "Yes, you!" I never shook it off—I couldn't! Ultimately, even though I could not see how God could ever use me I came to the firm conclusion that he was calling me. That fact I have never doubted.

There followed the long, somewhat trying years of preparation, including Bible school, college, and seminary. I began this period of preparation with a strong conviction that the Bible was the inspired Word of God and that conviction deepened as time went on. Through the years I have rejoiced in the integrity, dependability and authority of the Word of God.

Considering our personal weaknesses, our sins, and many mistakes, I assume it is rather natural for people to wish at times that they could go back and live their lives over again. I have never given much to retrospection or reminiscing. I have always been challenged by Paul's statement, "Forgetting those things which are behind, and reaching forth unto those things which are before." Yet I am sure there is real value in giving careful consideration to the way we respond to the stewardship of life. Therefore, I would do the following if I had my ministry to live over.

I would ask for nothing better than to have the privilege of serving as a pastor. To me there is no greater relationship in all the world (apart from family relationships) than that which exists between a pastor and his people. My wife and I rejoiced in it. From time to time other channels of service presented themselves but always we decided that the pastorate was our field. Only when I was within a couple of years of retirement did I feel that God's hand was very definitely calling me to serve as Metropolitan Missions Coordinator for the greater Los Angeles Area. It turned out to be a wonderfully rewarding opportunity.

I would make it my determined purpose always to

preach the Word. Believing so firmly that the Bible is infallible and inerrant, I always sought to preach it clearly and simply. However, looking back through the years I realize that I did a good deal of topical preaching. While I always sought to saturate these messages with passages of Scripture, I am convinced that the most effective type of preaching lies in expository preaching. I preached through the Word of God, chapter by chapter and book by book during the twelve years with the beloved First Baptist Church of Houston, Texas.

I would give less attention to a number of secondary activities. More time should be given to going where the people are and witnessing to them. My wife and I sought to visit together through the years. There can be no substitute for consistent, continual, untiring personal contact with people in their homes, places of business or wherever they can be found. I am sure that I allowed too much time to be occupied with things of lesser importance.

I would plan more carefully to give adequate time to my family. The emergencies among a congregation of people and the unexpected responsibilities always come, and the only way to maintain a satisfactory home life is to plan for it. I regret that I did not make this a primary consideration.

I would spend more time in personal Bible study and fellowship with the Lord. One of the temptations for every preacher is to study the Bible for what he can find in it for others rather than to let it speak to his own heart. I was not always the man I should have been because of a neglect of my own spiritual life.

I would seek to be more compassionate and tolerant. With sorrow I can see too much of the Pharisee within myself. I believe I would want to be more careful about passing judgment upon others and more willing to listen when they differ with me.

I would cultivate a closer fellowship with my younger preacher brethren. It has been an element in my ministry which has always been a source of joy. I have never had to force myself. It just seemed to come naturally. Many of my dearest preacher friends are less than half my own age. There is no generation gap between us. I have rejoiced to see them grow and develop and become fruitful leaders. It would be my hope that out of my own experiences and opportunities I might be able to contribute something to their lives that would result in greater honor to the Lord.

I would work with Southern Baptists. I am well aware that Southern Baptists have no corner on truth. I am conscious of our weaknesses as a Convention, as churches, and I am conscious of our weaknesses as individuals. I have not always agreed with the things that Southern Baptists have done, but I love them! They have been good to me. For over fifty years I have walked in their fellowship. From the beginning I felt a special kinship of spirit with Southern Baptists.

I glory in their loyalty to the Bible. I rejoice in the clear, positive personal gospel message they preach. I like their scriptural position with regard to the local church. Sometimes hands beckoned and voices called from other groups offering challenging opportunities for service. The decision was never difficult to make. I

am committed to the Southern Baptist way of life because I believe that God has appointed me a place
among them, and I am happy in it!

I would ask the Lord to forgive me for failing so many
times to put him first. I would ask him to remind me of
the words of John the Baptist concerning Jesus, namely,
"He must increase, I must decrease."

In conclusion as Mrs. White and I look back along the
road which we have traveled together for forty-nine
years we marvel at the grace of God extended to us.
Privileges and opportunities far beyond our dreams or
expectations came our way. I am grateful to the Lord for
my wife's faithful and consistent witness, for her love
for people and for her loyalty. I am grateful for all those
loving, patient, forgiving people who once called me
"Pastor" and whose support made the ministry of the
gospel a thing of joy in spite of the antagonism of the
world, the flesh, and the devil. Above all I am grateful
to the Lord who loved me, saved me, and called me into
his service.

I Would Conduct Fewer Revival Meetings as a Pastor

26

RICK INGLE, *evangelist*
Denton, Texas

In over three years of compiling all of the information of this book, I have read and reread each comment. Certainly I can say amen to each reflection. I have rededicated my life as a minister as I have been convicted of many errors in my own ministry.

Being a full-time Southern Baptist evangelist, and having this chapter bear the title, "I would conduct fewer revival meetings," may seem a strange response to the question of how I would change my ministry. However, I use this title as a pastor. My ministry is about evenly divided between being a full-time pastor and a full-time evangelist, having served ten years as a pastor and nearly that much time as an evangelist. I also noted that this subject was not written about by any other writer of this book.

Many times as a pastor I conducted as many as twelve revival meetings in one year. To be sure, several of these revival meetings were Monday through Saturday meetings, and did not take me from my church field during the weekdays. Nevertheless, a pastor can abuse his privileges and be away from his own church far too much. I confess this failing in my own pastoral ministry and if I could redo my pastoral ministry, I would conduct fewer revival meetings.

It is good for the pastor to be away in revival meetings. It is good for him and it is good for his church. The pastor can be refreshed and can get fired up all at the same time by conducting a revival meeting. Guest speakers are good for any church. However, there needs to be some discipline in deciding just how many meetings to conduct away from one's own pastorate. I know of one pastor who conducted as many as thirty revival campaigns in one year and still experienced growth in his own church. I will never know how he did it, but I am sure many pastoral duties went undone.

When people invite someone to attend their church, they want them to hear the pastor. There is no substitute for the pastor, regardless of who the guest speaker may be.

I would make it a point to be in my pulpit, and on the church field, the week before and the week after a revival meeting. This is a great shortcoming in the lives of many pastors. Having conducted over four hundred revival campaigns I witness this shortcoming often. The pastor needs to be in his pulpit and on the church field the week before a scheduled revival meeting making the proper preparation. And he certainly needs to be there the week following to lead out in the follow-up visitation. Many pastors leave their church field the week immediately following a revival meeting to conduct a revival meeting in another church. After a revival is not the time to leave the church to conduct a revival!

I believe all pastors ought to be pastor-evangelists. However, a man cannot be a full-time pastor and a full-time evangelist at the same time. I am afraid this is what I tried to be for many years while serving in the office of the pastor.

Dr. Lee Roberson is pastor of one of the largest churches in the world in Chattanooga, Tennessee, and yet he is never gone from his own pulpit on Wednesday or Sunday. Even when guest speakers are present he is there. Perhaps one of the reasons this church has baptized over 1,000 souls every year for over fifteen years, and has grown to be one of the largest churches in the world, is because the pastor is the pastor, not trying to be an evangelist at the same time.

If I had my pastoral ministry to live over I would conduct fewer revival meetings. I would stay on my church field, visit my own folks and the prospects for my church, and be a pastor to my people.